Presented to :

_____

From :

_____

Date :

_____

In these days of dark distress
Teach us to love more and hate less !

By

Helen Steiner Rice:

Heart Gifts

Lovingly

Prayerfully

Someone Cares

The Collected Poems of Helen Steiner Rice

Fleming H. Revell Company
Old Tappan, New Jersey

Library of Congress Cataloging in Publication Data

Rice, Helen Steiner.
  Someone cares.

  I. Title.
PS3568.I28S6   811'.5'4   75–186538
ISBN 0–8007–0524–6 (regular ed.)
ISBN 0–8007–0528–9 (boxed keepsake ed.)

The greatest need
in the world today is love...
More love for each other
and more love for God above!

Great is the Power
of Might and Mind
but Only Love
Can Make us Kind...
And Only Love
can completely fill
The Hearts of Men
with Peace and Goodwill!

Helen Steiner Rice

Contents

	The Power of Love	9
	A Word From the Publishers	11
1	He Loves You	13
2	Good Morning, God!	25
3	Help Yourself to Happiness	37
4	The Golden Chain of Friendship	47
5	Let God Bless Your Home	57
6	When Things Go Wrong	67
7	The Windows of Gold	83
8	The Light of the World	93
9	Life Is Forever	103
10	God Bless America	115
	This I Believe	123
	A Word From the Author	128

The Power of Love

There is no thinking person
    who can stand untouched today
And view the world around us
    drifting downward to decay
Without feeling deep within them
    a silent unnamed dread,
Wondering how to stem the chaos
    that lies frightfully ahead . . .
But the problems we are facing
    cannot humanly be solved
For our diplomatic strategy
    only gets us more involved
And our skillful ingenuity,
    our technology and science
Can never change a sinful heart
    filled with hatred and defiance . . .
So our problems keep on growing
    every hour of every day
As man vainly tries to solve them
    in his own SELF-WILLFUL WAY . . .
But man is powerless alone
    to CLEAN UP THE WORLD OUTSIDE
Until his own polluted soul
    is CLEAN and FREE INSIDE . . .
For the amazing power of love
    is beyond all comprehension
And it alone can heal this world
    of its hatred and dissension.

HELEN STEINER RICE

A Word From the Publishers

It is a pleasure and privilege to present this new book by Helen Steiner Rice, whose poems have brought comfort and hope to millions of readers around the world.

We are entering a world of computerized automation where only machines and numbers seem important. Yet all of us know that the only really important values are the human ones of trust and honor and love. These are the things Helen Steiner Rice cares deeply about, and these are the things emphasized in this new compilation of her verse, *Someone Cares.*

The author herself illustrates in many ways the fact that someone cares. Her poems always come to us in such immaculate condition that our own work is a joy. Above all she cares about people and God, as this book shows so clearly. She also cares enough about her readers to make every line instantly comprehensible; nothing she writes is obscure or ambiguous. While few people know what the average modern poet is trying to say, multitudes understand and love the work of Helen Steiner Rice.

Someone Cares! This book shows how important it is to find someone who does care, and to become a caring person. But it points supremely to the Someone above. Every poem by this author has an invisible vertical dimension that sets it apart from other verse. In addition to the poems there is a personal statement of faith by Mrs. Rice, entitled "This I Believe," which clearly reveals the spiritual dimension in her own life.

It is this spiritual dimension that gives the work of Helen Steiner Rice such universal appeal. Most of her books have sold better every year since publication—a rare event in the publishing world —indicating their tremendous ministry.

This new book, we are confident, will prove to be one of the most appealing and inspiring of all.

1

He Loves You

Someone Cares

Someone cares and always will,
The world forgets but God loves you still,
You cannot go beyond His Love
No matter what you're guilty of—
For God forgives until the end,
He is your faithful, loyal friend,
And though you try to hide your face
There is no shelter any place
That can escape His watchful eye,
For on the earth and in the sky
HE'S EVER PRESENT and ALWAYS THERE
To take you in His tender care
And bind the wounds and mend the breaks
When all the world around forsakes . . .
SOMEONE CARES and LOVES YOU STILL
And GOD is THE SOMEONE who always will.

✳ *God, Are You There?* ✳

I'm way down HERE!
You're way up THERE!
Are You sure You can hear
My faint, faltering prayer?
For I'm so unsure
Of just how to pray—
To tell You the truth, God,
I don't know what to say . . .
I just know I am lonely
And vaguely disturbed,
Bewildered and restless,
Confused and perturbed . . .
And they tell me that prayer
Helps to quiet the mind
And to unburden the heart
For in stillness we find
A newborn assurance
That SOMEONE DOES CARE
And SOMEONE DOES ANSWER
Each small sincere prayer!

Be of Good Cheer— There's Nothing to Fear!

Cheerful thoughts like sunbeams
Lighten up the "darkest fears"
For when the heart is happy
There's just no time for tears—
And when the face is smiling
It's impossible to frown,
And when you are "high-spirited"
You cannot feel "low-down"—
For the nature of our attitude
Toward circumstantial things
Determines our acceptance
Of the problems that life brings,
And since fear and dread and worry
Cannot help in any way,
It's much healthier and happier
To be cheerful every day—
And if you'll only try it
You will find, without a doubt,
A cheerful attitude's something
No one should be without—
For when the heart is cheerful
It cannot be filled with fear,
And without fear the way ahead
Seems more distinct and clear—
And we realize there's nothing
We need ever face alone
For our HEAVENLY FATHER loves us
And our problems are His own.

It's a Wonderful World

In spite of the fact
    we complain and lament
And view this old world
    with much discontent,
Deploring conditions
    and grumbling because
There's so much injustice
    and so many flaws,
It's a wonderful world
    and it's people like you ·
Who make it that way
    by the things that they do—
For a warm, ready smile
    or a kind, thoughtful deed,
Or a hand outstretched
    in an hour of need
Can change our whole outlook
    and make the world bright
Where a minute before
    just nothing seemed right—
It's a WONDERFUL WORLD
    and it always will be
If we keep our eyes open
    and focused to see
The WONDERFUL THINGS
    man is capable of
When he opens his heart
    to GOD and HIS LOVE.

The Legend of the Spider
and the Silken Strand
Held in God's Hand

There's an old Danish Legend
    with a lesson for us all
Of an ambitious spider
    and his rise and his fall,
Who wove his sheer web
    with intricate care
As it hung suspended
    somewhere in midair,
Then in soft, idle luxury
    he feasted each day
On the small, foolish insects
    he enticed as his prey,
Growing ever more arrogant
    and smug all the while
He lived like a "king"
    in self-satisfied style—
And gazing one day
    at the sheer strand suspended,
He said, "I don't need this,"
    so he recklessly rended
The strand that had held
    his web in its place
And with sudden swiftness
    the web crumpled in space—
And that was the end
    of the spider who grew
So arrogantly proud
    that he no longer knew

That it was the strand
    that reached down from above
Like the chord of God's grace
    and His infinite love
That links our lives
    to the great unknown,
For man cannot live
    or exist on his own—
And this old legend
    with simplicity told
Is a moral as true
    as the legend is old—
Don't sever the "lifeline"
    that links you to
THE FATHER IN HEAVEN
    WHO CARES FOR YOU.

He Loves You!

It's amazing and incredible,
But it's as true as it can be,
God loves and understands us all
And that means YOU and ME—
His grace is all sufficient
For both the YOUNG and OLD,
For the lonely and the timid,
For the brash and for the bold—
His love knows no exceptions,
So never feel excluded
No matter WHO or WHAT you are
Your name has been included—
And no matter what your past has been,
Trust God to understand,
And no matter what your problem is
Just place it in His Hand—
For in all of our UNLOVELINESS
This GREAT GOD LOVES US STILL,
He loved us since the world began
And what's more, HE ALWAYS WILL!

Warm Our Hearts With Thy Love

Oh, God, who made the summer
    and warmed the earth with beauty,
Warm our hearts with gratitude
    and devotion to our duty,
For in this age of violence,
    rebellion and defiance
We've forgotten the true meaning
    of "dependable reliance"—
We have lost our sense of duty
    and our sense of values, too,
And what was once unsanctioned,
    no longer is taboo,
Our standards have been lowered
    and we resist all discipline,
And our vision has been narrowed
    and blinded to all sin—
Oh, put the summer brightness
    in our closed, unseeing eyes
So in the careworn faces
    that we pass we'll recognize
The heartbreak and the loneliness,
    the trouble and despair
That a word of understanding
    would make easier to bear—
Oh, God, look down on our cold hearts
    and warm them with Your love,
And grant us Your forgiveness
    which we're so unworthy of.

Thank You, God, for Everything

Thank you, God, for everything—
    the big things and the small,
For "every good gift comes from God"—
    the giver of them all—
And all too often we accept
    without any thanks or praise
The gifts God sends as blessings
    each day in many ways,
And so at this THANKSGIVING TIME
    we offer up a prayer
To thank you, God, for giving us
    a lot more than our share . . .
First, thank you for the little things
    that often come our way,
The things we take for granted
    but don't mention when we pray,
The unexpected courtesy,
    the thoughtful, kindly deed,
A hand reached out to help us
    in the time of sudden need . . .
Oh, make us more aware, dear God,
    of little daily graces
That come to us with "sweet surprise"
    from never-dreamed-of places—
Then, thank you for the "MIRACLES"
    we are much too blind to see,
And give us new awareness
    of our many gifts from Thee,
And help us to remember
    that the KEY to LIFE and LIVING
Is to make each prayer a PRAYER of THANKS
    and every day THANKSGIVING.

Beyond Our Asking

More than hearts can imagine
    or minds comprehend,
God's bountiful gifts
    are ours without end—
We ask for a cupful
    when the vast sea is ours,
We pick a small rosebud
    from a garden of flowers,
We reach for a sunbeam
    but the sun still abides,
We draw one short breath
    but there's air on all sides—
Whatever we ask for
    falls short of God's giving
For HIS GREATNESS exceeds
    every facet of living,
And always God's ready
    and eager and willing
To pour out His mercy
    completely fulfilling
All of man's needs
    for peace, joy and rest
For God gives His children
    WHATEVER IS BEST—
Just give Him a chance
    to open HIS TREASURES
And He'll fill your life
    with unfathomable pleasures,
Pleasures that never
    grow worn-out and faded
And leave us depleted,
    disillusioned and jaded—
For God has a "storehouse"
    just filled to the brim
With all that man needs
    if we'll only ask Him.

What More Can You Ask *

God's love endureth forever—
What a wonderful thing to know
When the tides of life run against you
And your spirit is downcast and low . . .
God's kindness is ever around you,
Always ready to freely impart
Strength to your faltering spirit,
Cheer to your lonely heart . . .
God's presence is ever beside you,
As near as the reach of your hand,
You have but to tell Him your troubles,
There is nothing He won't understand . . .
And knowing God's love is unfailing,
And His mercy unending and great,
You have but to trust in His promise—
"God comes not too soon or too late" . . .
So wait with a heart that is patient
For the goodness of God to prevail—
For never do prayers go unanswered,
And His mercy and love never fail.

2

Good
Morning,
God !

Good Morning, God!

YOU are ushering in another day
Untouched and freshly new
So here I come to ask You, God,
If You'll renew me, too,
Forgive the many errors
That I made yesterday
And let me try again, dear God,
To walk closer in THY WAY . . .
But, Father, I am well aware
I can't make it on my own
So TAKE MY HAND and HOLD IT TIGHT
For I can't WALK ALONE!

The Peace
of Meditation

So we may know God better
    and feel His quiet power,
Let us daily keep in silence
    A MEDITATION HOUR—
For to understand God's greatness
    and to use His gifts each day
The soul must learn to meet Him
    in a meditative way,
For our Father tells His children
    that if they would know His will
They must seek Him in the silence
    when all is calm and still . . .
For nature's greatest forces
    are found in quiet things
Like softly falling snowflakes
    drifting down on angels' wings,
Or petals dropping soundlessly
    from a lovely full-blown rose,
So God comes closest to us
    when our souls are in repose . . .
So let us plan with prayerful care
    to always allocate
A certain portion of each day
    to be still and meditate . . .
For when everything is quiet
    and we're lost in meditation,
Our soul is then preparing
    for a deeper dedication
That will make it wholly possible
    to quietly endure
The violent world around us—
    for in God we are secure.

No Favor Do I Seek Today

I come not to ASK, to PLEAD or IMPLORE
  You,
I just come to tell You HOW MUCH I ADORE
  You,
For to kneel in Your Presence makes me feel blest
For I know that You know all my needs best . . .
And it fills me with joy just to linger with You
As my soul You replenish and my heart You
  renew,
For prayer is much more than just asking for
  things—
It's the PEACE and CONTENTMENT that
  QUIETNESS brings . . .
So thank You again for Your MERCY and LOVE
And for making me heir to YOUR KINGDOM
  ABOVE!

The Mystery of Prayer

Beyond that which words can interpret
Or theology can explain
The soul feels a "shower of refreshment"
That falls like the gentle rain
On hearts that are parched with problems
And are searching to find the way
To somehow attract God's attention
Through well-chosen words as they pray,
Not knowing that God in His wisdom
Can sense all man's worry and woe
For there is nothing man can conceal
That God does not already know . . .
So kneel in prayer in His presence
And you'll find no need to speak
For softly in silent communion
God grants you the peace that you seek.

It's Me Again, God

REMEMBER ME, GOD?
I come every day
Just to talk with You, Lord,
And to learn how to pray . . .
You make me feel welcome,
You reach out Your hand,
I need never explain
For YOU understand . . .
I come to You frightened
And burdened with care
So lonely and lost
And so filled with despair,
And suddenly, Lord,
I'm no longer afraid,
My burden is lighter
And the dark shadows fade . . .
Oh, God, what a comfort
To know that You care
And to know when I seek You
YOU WILL ALWAYS BE THERE!

✳ *What Is Prayer?* ✳

Is it measured words that are memorized,
Forcefully said and dramatized,
Offered with pomp and with arrogant pride
In words unmatched to the feelings inside?
No . . . prayer is so often just words unspoken
Whispered in tears by a heart that is broken . . .
For God is already deeply aware
Of the burdens we find too heavy to bear,
And all we need do is to seek Him in prayer
And without a word He will help us to bear
Our trials and troubles—our sickness and sorrow
And show us the way to a brighter tomorrow . . .
There's no need at all for IMPRESSIVE PRAYER
For the minute we seek God HE IS ALREADY
    THERE!

If You Meet God in the Morning, He'll Go With You Through the Day

"The earth is the Lord's
    and the fulness thereof"—
It speaks of His greatness,
    it sings of His love,
And each day at dawning
    I lift my heart high
And raise up my eyes
    to the infinite sky . . .
I watch the night vanish
    as a new day is born,
And I hear the birds sing
    on the wings of the morn,
I see the dew glisten
    in crystal-like splendor
While God, with a touch
    that is gentle and tender,
Wraps up the night
    and softly tucks it away
And hangs out the sun
    to herald a new day . . .
And so I give thanks
    and my heart kneels to pray—
"God, keep me and guide me
    and go with me today."

Make This Your Daily Prayer

Bless me, heavenly Father,
    forgive my erring ways,
Grant me strength to serve THEE,
    put purpose in my days . . .
Give me understanding
    enough to make me kind
So I may judge all people
    with my heart and not my mind . . .
And teach me to be patient
    in everything I do,
Content to trust YOUR wisdom
    and to follow after YOU . . .
And help me when I falter
    and hear me when I pray
And receive me in THY KINGDOM
    to dwell with THEE some day.

✳On the Wings
of Prayer✳

Just close your eyes
    and open your heart
And feel your worries
    and cares depart,
Just yield yourself
    to the Father above
And let Him hold you
    secure in His love . . .
For life on earth
    grows more involved
With endless problems
    that can't be solved—
But God only asks us
    to do our best,
Then He will "take over"
    and finish the rest . . .
So when you are tired,
    discouraged and blue,
There's always one door
    that is open to you—
And that is the door
    to "THE HOUSE OF PRAYER"
And you'll find God waiting
    to meet you there . . .
And "THE HOUSE OF PRAYER"
    is no farther away
Than the quiet spot
    where you kneel and pray—
For the heart is a temple
    when God is there
As we place ourselves
    in His loving care,

And He hears every prayer
 and answers each one
When we pray in His name
 "THY WILL BE DONE"—
And the burdens that seemed
 too heavy to bear
Are lifted away
 on "THE WINGS OF PRAYER."

✳ No Prayer Goes Unheard ✳

Often we pause and wonder
When we kneel down to pray—
Can God really hear
The prayers that we say . . .
But if we keep praying
And talking to Him,
He'll brighten the soul
That was clouded and dim,
And as we continue
Our burden seems lighter,
Our sorrow is softened
And our outlook is brighter—
For though we feel helpless
And alone when we start,
Our prayer is the key
That opens the heart,
And as our heart opens
The dear Lord comes in
And the prayer that we felt
We could never begin
Is so easy to say
For the Lord understands
And gives us new strength
By the touch of His hands.

Now I Lay Me Down to Sleep

I remember so well this prayer I said
Each night as my Mother tucked me in bed,
And today this same prayer is still the best way
To "sign off with God" at the end of the day
And to ask Him your soul to safely keep
As you wearily close tired eyes in sleep
Feeling content that The Father Above
Will hold you secure in His great arms of love . . .
And having His promise that if 'ere you wake
His angels will reach down your sweet soul to take
Is perfect assurance that awake or asleep
God is always right there to tenderly keep
ALL of HIS CHILDREN ever SAFE in HIS CARE
For God's HERE and He's THERE and He's
      EVERYWHERE . . .
So into His hands each night as I sleep
I commit my soul for the dear Lord to keep
Knowing that if my soul should take flight
It will soar to "THE LAND WHERE THERE
      IS NO NIGHT."

3

Help Yourself
to Happiness

The World Would Be a Nicer Place If We Traveled at a Slower Pace

Amid stresses and strains
    much too many to mention,
And pressure-packed days
    filled with turmoil and tension,
We seldom have time
    to be "FRIENDLY OR KIND"
For we're harassed and hurried
    and always behind—
And while we've more "gadgets"
    and "buttons to press"
Making leisure hours greater
    and laboring hours less,
And our standards of living
    they claim have improved
And "repressed inhibitions"
    have been freed and removed,
It seems all this PROGRESS
    and GROWTH are for naught,
For daily we see
    a WORLD MORE DISTRAUGHT—
So what does it matter
    if man reaches his goal
"And gains the whole world
    but loses his soul"—
For what have we won
    if in gaining this end
We've been much too busy
    to be KIND TO A FRIEND,
And what is there left
    to make the heart sing
When life is a COLD
    and MECHANICAL THING

And we are but puppets
of controlled automation
Instead of "joint heirs"
to "GOD'S GIFT OF CREATION."

✳ *Help Yourself to Happiness* ✳

Everybody, everywhere
seeks happiness, it's true,
But finding it and keeping it
seems difficult to do,
Difficult because we think
that happiness is found
Only in the places where
wealth and fame abound—
And so we go on searching
in "palaces of pleasure"
Seeking recognition
and monetary treasure,
Unaware that happiness
is just a "state of mind"
Within the reach of everyone
who takes time to be kind—
For in making OTHERS HAPPY
we will be happy, too,
For the happiness you give away
returns to "shine on you."

He Asks So Little and Gives So Much

WHAT MUST I DO
    to insure peace of mind?
Is the answer I'm seeking
    too hard to find?
HOW CAN I KNOW
    what God wants me to be?
HOW CAN I TELL
    what's expected of me?
WHERE CAN I GO
    for guidance and aid
To help me correct
    the errors I've made?
The answer is found
    in doing THREE THINGS
And great is the gladness
    that doing them brings . . .
"DO JUSTICE"—"LOVE KINDNESS"—
    "WALK HUMBLY WITH GOD"—
For with these THREE THINGS
    as your "rule and your rod"
All things worth having
    are yours to achieve
If you follow God's words
    and have FAITH TO BELIEVE!

Things to Be Thankful For

The good, green earth beneath our feet,
The air we breathe, the food we eat,
Some work to do, a goal to win,
A hidden longing deep within
That spurs us on to bigger things
And helps us meet what each day brings,
All these things and many more
Are things we should be thankful for . . .
And most of all our thankful prayers
Should rise to God because He cares!

A Favorite Recipe

Take a CUP of KINDNESS,
    mix it well with LOVE,
Add a lot of Patience
    and FAITH in GOD ABOVE,
Sprinkle very generously
    with JOY and THANKS and CHEER—
And you'll have lots of "ANGEL FOOD"
    to feast on all the year.

✳ Look on the Sunny Side ✳

There are always two sides,
    the GOOD and the BAD,
The DARK and the LIGHT,
    the SAD and the GLAD—
But in looking back over
    the GOOD and the BAD
We're aware of the number
    of GOOD THINGS we've had—
And in counting our blessings
    we find when we're through
We've no reason at all
    to complain or be blue—
So thank God for GOOD things
    He has already done,
And be grateful to Him
    for the battles you've won,
And know that the same God
    who helped you before
Is ready and willing
    to help you once more—
Then with faith in your heart
    reach out for God's Hand
And accept what He sends,
    though you can't understand—
For OUR FATHER in heaven
    always knows what is best,
And if you trust in His wisdom
    your life will be blest,
For always remember
    that whatever betide you,
You are never alone
    for God is beside you.

A Sure Way to a Happy Day

HAPPINESS is something
    we create in our mind,
It's not something you search for
    and so seldom find—
It's just waking up
    and beginning the day
By counting our blessings
    and kneeling to pray—
It's giving up thoughts
    that breed discontent
And accepting what comes
    as a "gift heaven-sent"—
It's giving up wishing
    for things we have not
And making the best of
    whatever we've got—
It's knowing that life
    is determined for us,
And pursuing our tasks
    without fret, fume or fuss—
For it's by completing
    what God gives us to do
That we find real contentment
    and happiness, too.

Brighten the Corner Where You Are

We cannot all be famous
    or be listed in "WHO'S WHO,"
But every person great or small
    has important work to do,
For seldom do we realize
    the importance of small deeds
Or to what degree of greatness
    unnoticed kindness leads—
For it's not the big celebrity
    in a world of fame and praise,
But it's doing unpretentiously
    in undistinguished ways
The work that God assigned to us,
    unimportant as it seems,
That makes our task outstanding
    and brings reality to dreams—
So do not sit and idly wish
    for wider, new dimensions
Where you can put in practice
    your many "GOOD INTENTIONS"—
But at the spot God placed you
    begin at once to do
Little things to brighten up
    the lives surrounding you,
For if everybody brightened up
    the spot on which they're standing
By being more considerate
    and a little less demanding,
This dark old world would very soon
    eclipse the "Evening Star"
If everybody BRIGHTENED UP
    THE CORNER WHERE THEY ARE!

A Thankful Heart

Take nothing for granted,
    for whenever you do
The "joy of enjoying"
    is lessened for you—
For we rob our own lives
    much more than we know
When we fail to respond
    or in any way show
Our thanks for the blessings
    that daily are ours . . .
The warmth of the sun,
    the fragrance of flowers,
The beauty of twilight,
    the freshness of dawn,
The coolness of dew
    on a green velvet lawn,
The kind little deeds
    so thoughtfully done,
The favors of friends
    and the love that someone
Unselfishly gives us
    in a myriad of ways,
Expecting no payment
    and no words of praise—
Oh, great is our loss
    when we no longer find
A thankful response
    to things of this kind,
For the JOY OF ENJOYING
    and the FULLNESS OF LIVING
Are found in the heart
    that is filled with THANKSGIVING.

Make Your Day Bright
by Thinking Right

Don't start your day by supposin'
    that trouble is just ahead,
It's better to stop supposin'
    and start with a prayer instead,
And make it a prayer of THANKSGIVING
    for the wonderful things God has wrought
Like the beautiful sunrise and sunset,
    "GOD'S GIFTS" that are free
    and not bought—
For what is the use of supposin'
    the dire things that could happen to you
And worry about some misfortune
    that seldom if ever comes true—
But instead of just idle supposin'
    step forward to meet each new day
Secure in the knowledge God's near you
    to lead you each step of the way—
For supposin' the worst things will happen
    only helps to make them come true
And you darken the bright, happy moments
    that the dear Lord has given to you—
So if you desire to be happy
    and get rid of the "MISERY of DREAD"
Just give up "SUPPOSIN' THE WORST THINGS"
    and look for "THE BEST THINGS" instead.

4

The Golden Chain of Friendship

The Golden Chain
of Friendship

FRIENDSHIP is a GOLDEN CHAIN,
The links are friends so dear,
And like a rare and precious jewel
It's treasured more each year . . .
It's clasped together firmly
With a love that's deep and true,
And it's rich with happy memories
And fond recollections, too . . .

Time can't destroy its beauty
For, as long as memory lives,
Years can't erase the pleasure
That the joy of friendship gives . . .
For friendship is a priceless gift
That can't be bought or sold,
But to have an understanding friend
Is worth far more than gold . . .
And the GOLDEN CHAIN of FRIENDSHIP
Is a strong and blessed tie
Binding kindred hearts together
As the years go passing by.

The Gift of Friendship *

FRIENDSHIP is a PRICELESS GIFT
    that cannot be bought or sold,
But its value is far greater
    than a mountain made of gold—
For gold is cold and lifeless,
    it can neither see nor hear,
And in the time of trouble
    it is powerless to cheer—
It has no ears to listen,
    no heart to understand,
It cannot bring you comfort
    or reach out a helping hand—
So when you ask God for a GIFT,
    be thankful if HE sends
Not diamonds, pearls or riches,
    but the love of real true friends.

Give Us Daily Awareness

On life's busy thoroughfares
We meet with angels unawares—
So, Father, make us kind and wise
So we may always recognize
The blessings that are ours to take,
The friendships that are ours to make
If we but open our heart's door wide
To let the sunshine of love inside.

The Key to Living Is Giving!

A very favorite story of mine
    is about TWO SEAS IN PALESTINE—

One is a sparkling sapphire jewel,
    its waters are clean and clear and cool,
Along its shores the children play
    and travelers seek it on their way,
And nature gives so lavishly
    her choicest gems to the GALILEE . . .
But on to the south the Jordan flows
    into a sea where nothing grows,
No splash of fish, no singing bird,
    no children's laughter is ever heard,
The air hangs heavy all around
    and nature shuns this barren ground . . .
Both seas receive the Jordan's flow,
    the water is just the same, we know,
But one of the seas, like liquid sun,
    can warm the hearts of everyone,
While farther south another sea
    is dead and dark and miserly—
It takes each drop the Jordan brings
    and to each drop it fiercely clings . . .
It hoards and holds the Jordan's waves
    until like shackled, captured slaves
The fresh, clear Jordan turns to salt
    and dies within the DEAD SEA'S vault . . .
But the Jordan flows on rapturously
    as it enters and leaves the GALILEE,
For every drop that the Jordan gives
    becomes a laughing wave that lives—
For the GALILEE gives back each drop,
    its waters flow and never stop,
And in this laughing, living sea
    that takes and gives so generously

We find the way to LIFE and LIVING
    is not in KEEPING, but in GIVING!

Yes, there are TWO PALESTINIAN SEAS
    and mankind is fashioned after these!

Strangers Are Friends We Haven't Met

God knows NO STRANGERS, He loves us all,
    the poor, the rich, the great, the small . . .
He is a friend who is always there
    to share our troubles and lessen our care . . .
No one is a stranger in God's sight,
    for GOD IS LOVE and in HIS LIGHT
May we, too, try in our small way
    to make NEW FRIENDS from day to day . . .
So pass no stranger with an unseeing eye,
    for God may be sending A NEW FRIEND
    BY.

A Friend Is a Gift of God

Among the great and glorious gifts
    our heavenly Father sends
Is the GIFT of UNDERSTANDING
    that we find in loving friends,
For in this world of trouble
    that is filled with anxious care
Everybody needs a friend
    in whom they're free to share
The little secret heartaches
    that lay heavy on their mind,
Not just a mere acquaintance
    but someone who's "JUST OUR KIND"—
For, somehow, in the generous heart
    of loving, faithful friends
The good God in His charity
    and wisdom always sends
A sense of understanding
    and the power of perception
And mixes these fine qualities
    with kindness and affection
So when we need some sympathy
    or a friendly hand to touch,
Or an ear that listens tenderly
    and speaks words that mean so much,
We seek our true and trusted friend
    in the knowledge that we'll find
A heart that's sympathetic
    and an understanding mind. . . .
And often just without a word
    there seems to be a union
Of thoughts and kindred feelings
    for GOD gives TRUE FRIENDS communion.

The Soul of Man

Every man has a deep heart need
  that cannot be filled with doctrine or creed,
For the soul of man knows nothing more
  than just that he is longing for
A haven that is safe and sure,
  a fortress where he feels secure,
An island in this sea of strife
  away from all the storms of life . . .
Oh, God of love, who sees us all,
  You are SO GREAT! We are so small!
Hear man's universal prayer
  crying to You in despair—
"Save my soul and grant me peace,
  let my restless murmurings cease,
God of love—Forgive! Forgive!
  teach me how to TRULY LIVE,
Ask me not my race or creed,
  just take me in my hour of need,
And let me know You love me, too,
  and that I am A PART OF YOU" . . .
And someday may man realize
  that all the earth, the seas and skies
Belong to God who made us all,
  the rich, the poor, the great, the small,
And in the Father's Holy Sight
  no man is yellow, black or white,
And PEACE ON EARTH cannot be found
  until we MEET ON COMMON GROUND
And every man becomes a BROTHER
  who worships God and loves each other.

53

Give Lavishly!
Live Abundantly!

The more you give, the more you get—
The more you laugh, the less you fret—
The more you do UNSELFISHLY,
The more you live ABUNDANTLY . . .

The more of everything you share,
The more you'll always have to spare—
The more you love, the more you'll find
That life is good and friends are kind . . .

For only WHAT WE GIVE AWAY,
ENRICHES US FROM DAY TO DAY.

"Flowers Leave Their Fragrance on the Hand That Bestows Them"

There's an old Chinese proverb
    that, if practiced each day,
Would change the whole world
    in a wonderful way—
Its truth is so simple,
    it's so easy to do,
And it works every time
    and successfully, too . . .
For you can't do a kindness
    without a reward,
Not in silver nor gold
    but in joy from the Lord—
You can't light a candle
    to show others the way
Without feeling the warmth
    of that bright little ray . . .
And you can't pluck a rose,
    all fragrant with dew,
Without part of its fragrance
    remaining with you.

Everyone Needs Someone

People need people
    and friends need friends,
And we all need love
    for a full life depends
Not on vast riches
    or great acclaim,
Not on success
    or on worldly fame,
But just in knowing
    that someone cares
And holds us close
    in their thoughts and prayers—
For only the knowledge
    that we're understood
Makes everyday living
    feel WONDERFULLY GOOD,
And we rob ourselves
    of life's greatest need
When we "lock up our hearts"
    and fail to heed
The outstretched hand
    reaching to find
A kindred spirit
    whose heart and mind
Are lonely and longing
    to somehow share
Our joys and sorrows
    and to make us aware
That life's completeness
    and richness depends
On the things we share
    with our loved ones and friends.

5

Let God
Bless Your
Home

✳ The Magic of Love ✳

LOVE is like MAGIC
And it always will be,
For love still remains
LIFE'S SWEET MYSTERY!
LOVE works in ways
That are wondrous and strange
And there's NOTHING IN LIFE
That LOVE CANNOT CHANGE!
LOVE can transform
The most commonplace
Into beauty and splendor
And sweetness and grace!
LOVE is unselfish,
Understanding and kind,
For it sees with its HEART
And not with its mind!
LOVE is the answer
That everyone seeks—
LOVE is the language
That every heart speaks—
LOVE can't be bought,
It is priceless and free,
LOVE like pure MAGIC
Is a SWEET MYSTERY!

When Two People Marry

Your hearts are filled with happiness
    so great and overflowing,
You cannot comprehend it
    for it's far beyond all knowing
How any heart could hold such joy
    or feel the fullness of
The wonder and the glory
    and the ecstasy of love—
You wish that you could capture it
    and never let it go
So you might walk forever
    in its radiant magic glow . . .
But love in all its ecstasy
    is such a fragile thing,
Like gossamer in cloudless skies
    or a hummingbird's small wing,
But love that lasts FOREVER
    must be made of something strong,
The kind of strength that's gathered
    when the heart can hear no song—
When the "sunshine" of your wedding day
    runs into "stormy weather"
And hand in hand you brave the gale
    and climb steep hills together,
And clinging to each other
    while the thunder rolls above
You seek divine protection
    in FAITH and HOPE and LOVE . . .
For "DAYS OF WINE AND ROSES"
    never make love's dream come true,
It takes sacrifice and teardrops,
    and problems shared by two,
To give true love its BEAUTY,
    its GRANDEUR and its FINENESS
And to mold an "earthly ecstasy"
    into HEAVENLY DIVINENESS.

Where There Is Love

Where there is love the heart is light,
Where there is love the day is bright,
Where there is love there is a song
To help when things are going wrong . . .
Where there is love there is a smile
To make all things seem more worthwhile,
Where there is love there's quiet peace,
A tranquil place where turmoils cease—
Love changes darkness into light
And makes the heart take "wingless flight" . . .
Oh, blest are they who walk in love,
They also walk with God above—
And when you walk with God each day
And kneel together when you pray,
Your marriage will be truly blest
And God will be your daily "GUEST"—
And love that once seemed yours alone,
God gently blends into HIS OWN.

Love One Another, for Love Is of God

Every couple should remember
 that what the world calls love
Is not something man invented,
 but it comes from God above . . .
And love can be neglected
 and oftentimes abused,
Perverted and distorted,
 misguided and misused,
Or it can be developed
 by living every day
Near to God, OUR FATHER,
 and following in HIS WAY . . .
For God alone can teach you
 the meaning of true love,
And He can help establish
 the life you're dreaming of
In which you live together
 in happiness and peace,
Enjoying married blessings
 that day by day increase . . .
For love that is immortal
 has its source in God above,
And the love you give each other
 is founded on His love . . .
And though upon YOUR WEDDING DAY
 it seems YOURS and YOURS ALONE,
If you but ask, God takes YOUR LOVE
 and blends it with HIS OWN.

What Is Marriage? *

Marriage is the union
    of two people in love,
And love is sheer magic
    for it's woven of
Gossamer dreams,
    enchantingly real,
That people in love
    are privileged to feel—
But the "exquisite ecstasy"
    that captures the heart
Of two people in love
    is just a small part
Of the beauty and wonder
    and MIRACLE of
The growth and fulfillment
    and evolvement of love—
For only long years
    of living together
And sharing and caring
    in all kinds of weather
Both pleasure and pain,
    the glad and the sad,
Teardrops and laughter,
    the good and the bad,
Can add new dimensions
    and lift love above
The rapturous ecstasies
    of "falling in love"—
For ecstasy passes
    but it is replaced
By something much greater
    that cannot be defaced,
For what was "in part"
    has now "become whole"—
For on the "wings of the flesh,"
    love entered the "soul"!

Fathers Are Wonderful People

Fathers are wonderful people
    too little understood,
And we do not sing their praises
    as often as we should . . .
For, somehow, Father seems to be
    the man who pays the bills,
While Mother binds up little hurts
    and nurses all our ills . . .
And Father struggles daily
    to live up to "HIS IMAGE"
As protector and provider
    and "hero of the scrimmage" . . .
And perhaps that is the reason
    we sometimes get the notion
That Fathers are not subject
    to the thing we call emotion,
But if you look inside Dad's heart,
    where no one else can see,
You'll find he's sentimental
    and as "soft" as he can be . . .
But he's so busy every day
    in the gruelling race of life,
He leaves the sentimental stuff
    to his partner and his wife . . .
But Fathers are just WONDERFUL
    in a million different ways,
And they merit loving compliments
    and accolades of praise,
For the only reason Dad aspires
    to fortune and success
Is to make the family proud of him
    and to bring them happiness . . .
And like OUR HEAVENLY FATHER,
    he's a guardian and a guide,
Someone that we can count on
    to be ALWAYS ON OUR SIDE.

What Is a Mother

It takes a Mother's LOVE to make a house a home,
A place to be remembered, no matter where we
    roam . . .
It takes a Mother's PATIENCE to bring a child
    up right,
And her COURAGE and her CHEERFULNESS
    to make a dark day bright . . .
It takes a Mother's THOUGHTFULNESS to
    mend the heart's deep "hurts,"
And her SKILL and her ENDURANCE to mend
    little socks and shirts . . .
It takes a Mother's KINDNESS to forgive us when
    we err,
To sympathize in trouble and bow her head in
    prayer . . .
It takes a Mother's WISDOM to recognize our
    needs
And to give us reassurance by her loving words
    and deeds . . .
It takes a Mother's ENDLESS FAITH, her CON-
    FIDENCE and TRUST
To guide us through the pitfalls of selfishness and
    lust . . .
And that is why in all this world there could not
    be another
Who could fulfill God's purpose as completely as a
    MOTHER!

A Mother's Love

A Mother's love is something
    that no one can explain,
It is made of deep devotion
    and of sacrifice and pain,
It is endless and unselfish
    and enduring come what may
For nothing can destroy it
    or take that love away . . .
It is patient and forgiving
    when all others are forsaking,
And it never fails or falters
    even though the heart is breaking . . .
It believes beyond believing
    when the world around condemns,
And it glows with all the beauty
    of the rarest, brightest gems . . .
It is far beyond defining,
    it defies all explanation,
And it still remains a secret
    like the mysteries of creation . . .
A many splendored miracle
    man cannot understand
And another wondrous evidence
    of God's tender guiding hand.

Life's Golden Autumn

BIRTHDAYS come and BIRTHDAYS go
    and with them comes the thought
Of all the happy MEMORIES
    that the passing years have brought—
And looking back across the years
    it's a joy to reminisce,
For MEMORY OPENS WIDE THE DOOR
    on a happy day like this,
And with a sweet nostalgia
    we longingly recall
The HAPPY DAYS OF LONG AGO
    that seem the BEST OF ALL—
But TIME cannot be halted
    in its swift and endless flight
And AGE is sure to follow YOUTH
    as DAY comes after NIGHT—
And once again it's proven
    that the restless brain of man
Is powerless to alter
    GOD'S GREAT UNCHANGING PLAN—
But while our step grows slower
    and we grow more tired, too,
The SOUL goes soaring UPWARD
    to realms untouched and new,
For growing older only means
    the SPIRIT grows serene
And we behold things with OUR SOULS
    that our eyes have never seen—
And BIRTHDAYS are but GATEWAYS
    to ETERNAL LIFE ABOVE
Where "God's children" live FOREVER
    in the BEAUTY of HIS LOVE.

6

When Things
Go Wrong

Let Go and Let God!

When you're troubled and worried and sick at heart
And your plans are upset and your world falls apart,
Remember God's ready and waiting to share
The burden you find much too heavy to bear—
So with faith, "LET GO" and "LET GOD" lead the way
Into a brighter and less troubled day.

After the Winter... God Sends the Spring

Springtime is a season
    of HOPE and JOY and CHEER,
There's beauty all around us
    to see and touch and hear . . .
So, no matter how downhearted
    and discouraged we may be,
New Hope is born when we behold
    leaves budding on a tree . . .
Or when we see a timid flower
    push through the frozen sod
And open wide in glad surprise
    its petaled eyes to God . . .
For this is just God saying—
    "Lift up your eyes to Me,
And the bleakness of your spirit,
    like the budding springtime tree,
Will lose its wintry darkness
    and your heavy heart will sing"—
For God never sends THE WINTER
    without the JOY OF SPRING.

How Great the Yield From a Fertile Field

The farmer ploughs through the fields of green
And the blade of the plough is sharp and keen,
But the seed must be sown to bring forth grain,
For nothing is born without suffering and pain—
And God never ploughs in the soul of man
Without intention and purpose and plan,
So whenever you feel the plough's sharp blade
Let not your heart be sorely afraid
For, like the farmer, God chooses a field
From which He expects an excellent yield—
So rejoice though your heart is broken in two,
God seeks to bring forth a rich harvest in you.

There Are Blessings in Everything

Blessings come in many guises
 That God alone in love devises,
And sickness which we dread so much
 Can bring a very "healing touch"—
For often on the "wings of pain"
 The peace we sought before in vain
Will come to us with "sweet surprise"
 For God is merciful and wise—
And through long hours of tribulation
 God gives us time for meditation,
And no sickness can be counted loss
 That teaches us to "bear our cross."

Great Faith That Smiles Is Born of Great Trials

It's easy to say "IN GOD WE TRUST"
When life is radiant and fair,
But the test of faith is only found
When there are burdens to bear—
For our claim to faith in the "sunshine"
Is really NO FAITH AT ALL,
For when roads are smooth and days are bright
Our need for God is so small,
And no one discovers the fullness
Or the greatness of God's love
Unless they have walked in the "darkness"
With only a LIGHT from ABOVE—
For the faith to endure whatever comes
Is born of sorrow and trials,
And strengthened only by discipline
And nurtured by self-denials—
So be not disheartened by troubles,
For trials are the "building blocks"
On which to erect a FORTRESS of FAITH
Secure on God's "ageless rocks."

Trouble Is a
Stepping-Stone
to Growth

Trouble is something no one can escape,
Everyone has it in some form or shape—
Some people hide it 'way down deep inside,
Some people bear it with gallant-like pride,
Some people worry and complain of their lot,
Some people covet what they haven't got,
While others rebel and become bitter and old
With hopes that are dead and hearts that are cold . . .
But the wise man accepts whatever God sends,
Willing to yield like a storm-tossed tree bends,
Knowing that God never makes a mistake,
So whatever He sends they are willing to take—
For trouble is part and parcel of life
And no man can grow without trouble and strife,
And the steep hills ahead and high mountain peaks
Afford man at last the peace that he seeks—
So blest are the people who learn to accept
The trouble men try to escape and reject,
For in OUR ACCEPTANCE we're given great grace
And courage and faith and the strength to face
The daily troubles that come to us all
So we may learn to stand "straight and tall"—
For the grandeur of life is born of defeat
For in overcoming we make life complete.

Before You Can Dry Another's Tears— You Too Must Weep!

Let me not live a life that's free
From "THE THINGS" that draw me close to
     THEE—
For how can I ever hope to heal
The wounds of others I do not feel—
If my eyes are dry and I never weep,
How do I know when the hurt is deep—
If my heart is cold and it never bleeds,
How can I tell what my brother needs—
For when ears are deaf to the beggar's plea
And we close our eyes and refuse to see,
And we steel our hearts and harden our mind,
And we count it a weakness whenever we're kind,
We are no longer following THE FATHER'S WAY
Or seeking His guidance from day to day—
For, without "crosses to carry" and "burdens to
     bear,"
We dance through a life that is frothy and fair,
And "chasing the rainbow" we have no desire
For "roads that are rough" and "realms that are
     higher"—
So spare me no heartache or sorrow, dear Lord,
For the heart that is hurt reaps the richest reward,
And God enters the heart that is broken with sorrow
As He opens the door to a BRIGHTER
     TOMORROW,
For only through tears can we recognize
The suffering that lies in another's eyes.

Dark Shadows Fall
in the Lives of Us All

Sickness and sorrow come to us all,
But through it we grow and learn to "stand tall"—
For trouble is "part and parcel of life"
And no man can grow without struggle and strife,
And the more we endure with patience and grace
The stronger we grow and the more we can face—
And the more we can face, the greater our love,
And with love in our hearts we are more conscious of
The pain and the sorrow in lives everywhere,
So it is through trouble that we learn how to share.

This Too Will
Pass Away

If I can endure for this minute
Whatever is happening to me,
No matter how heavy my heart is
Or how "dark" the moment may be—
If I can but keep on believing
What I know in my heart to be true,
That "darkness will fade with the morning"
And that THIS WILL PASS AWAY, TOO—
Then nothing can ever disturb me
Or fill me with uncertain fear
For as sure as NIGHT BRINGS THE DAWNING
"MY MORNING" is bound to appear.

Count Your Gains
and Not Your Losses

As we travel down life's busy road
    complaining of our heavy load,
We often think God's been unfair
    and gave us much more than our share
Of little daily irritations
    and disappointing tribulations . . .
We're discontented with our lot
    and all the "bad breaks" that we got,
We count our losses, not our gain,
    and remember only tears and pain . . .
The good things we forget completely
    when God looked down and blessed us
      sweetly,
Our troubles fill our every thought,
    we dwell upon lost goals we sought,
And wrapped up in our own despair
    we have no time to see or share
Another's load that far outweighs
    our little problems and dismays . . .
And so we walk with head held low
    and little do we guess or know
That someone near us on life's street
    is burdened deeply with defeat . . .
But if we'd but forget OUR CARE
    and stop in sympathy to share
The burden that "our brother" carried,
    our mind and heart would be less harried
And we would feel our load was small,
    in fact, WE CARRIED NO LOAD AT ALL.

When Trouble Comes and Things Go Wrong!

Let us go quietly to God
    when trouble comes to us,
Let us never stop to whimper
    or complain and fret and fuss,
Let us hide "our thorns" in "roses"
    and "our sighs" in "golden song"
And "our crosses" in a "crown of smiles"
    whenever things go wrong . . .
For no one can really help us
    as our troubles we bemoan,
For COMFORT, HELP and INNER PEACE
    MUST COME FROM GOD ALONE . . .
So do not tell your neighbor,
    your companion or your friend
In the hope that they can help you
    bring your troubles to an end . . .
For they, too, have their problems,
    they are burdened just like you,
SO TAKE YOUR CROSS TO JESUS
    and HE WILL SEE YOU THROUGH . . .
And waste no time in crying
    on the shoulder of a friend
But go directly to the Lord
    for on Him you can depend . . .
For there's absolutely NOTHING
    that His mighty hand can't do
And He never is too busy
    to help and comfort you.

Today's Joy Was Born of Yesterday's Sorrow

Who said the "darkness of the night"
    would never turn to day,
Who said the "winter's bleakness"
    would never pass away,
Who said the fog would never lift
    and let the sunshine through,
Who said the skies now overcast
    would nevermore be blue—
Why should we ever entertain
    these thoughts so dark and grim
And let the brightness of our mind
    grow cynical and dim
When we know beyond all questioning
    that winter turns to spring
And on the notes of sorrow
    new songs are made to sing—
For no one sheds a teardrop
    or suffers loss in vain,
For God is always there to turn
    our losses into gain,
And every burden born TODAY
    and every present sorrow
Are but God's happy harbingers
    of a joyous, bright TOMORROW.

The Way to God

If my days were untroubled
    and my heart always light
Would I seek that fair land
    where there is no night?
If I never grew weary
    with the weight of my load
Would I search for God's Peace
    at the end of the road?
If I never knew sickness
    and never felt pain
Would I reach for a hand
    to help and sustain?
If I walked not with sorrow
    and lived without loss
Would my soul seek sweet solace
    at the foot of the cross?
If all I desired was mine
    day by day
Would I kneel before God
    and earnestly pray?
If God sent no "WINTER"
    to freeze me with fear
Would I yearn for the warmth
    of "SPRING" every year?
I ask myself this
    and the answer is plain—
If my life were all pleasure
    and I never knew pain
I'd seek God less often
    and need Him much less,
For God's sought more often
    in times of distress,
And no one knows God
    or sees Him as plain
As those who have met Him
    on "THE PATHWAY OF PAIN."

Never Borrow Sorrow From Tomorrow

Deal only with the present,
Never step into tomorrow,
For God asks us just to trust Him
And to never borrow sorrow—
For the future is not ours to know
And it may never be,
So let us live and give our best
And give it lavishly—
For to meet tomorrow's troubles
Before they are even ours
Is to anticipate the Saviour
And to doubt His all-wise powers—
So let us be content to solve
Our problems one by one,
Asking nothing of tomorrow
Except "Thy Will Be Done."

The Story of the Fire Lily

The crackling flames rise skyward
    as the waving grass is burned,
But from the fire on the veld
    a great truth can be learned . . .
For the green and living hillside
    becomes a funeral pyre
As all the grass across the veld
    is swallowed by the fire . . .
What yesterday was living,
    today is dead and still,
But soon a breathless miracle
    takes place upon the hill . . .
For, from the blackened ruins
    there arises life anew
And scarlet lilies lift their heads
    where once the veld grass grew . . .
And so again the mystery
    of life and death is wrought,
And man can find assurance
    in this soul-inspiring thought,
That from a bed of ashes
    the fire lilies grew,
And from the ashes of our lives
    God resurrects us, too.

It Takes the Bitter and the Sweet to Make a Life Full and Complete

Life is a mixture
    of sunshine and rain,
Laughter and teardrops,
    pleasure and pain—
Low tides and high tides,
    mountains and plains,
Triumphs, defeats
    and losses and gains—
But ALWAYS in ALL WAYS
    God's guiding and leading
And He alone knows
    the things we're most needing—
And when He sends sorrow
    or some dreaded affliction,
Be assured that it comes
    with God's kind benediction—
And if we accept it
    as a GIFT OF HIS LOVE,
We'll be showered with blessings
    from OUR FATHER ABOVE.

Let Not Your Heart Be Troubled

Whenever I am troubled
    and lost in deep despair
I bundle all my troubles up
    and go to God in prayer . . .

I tell Him I am heartsick
    and lost and lonely, too,
That my mind is deeply burdened
    and I don't know what to do . . .

But I know He stilled the tempest
    and calmed the angry sea
And I humbly ask if in His love
    He'll do the same for me . . .

And then I just keep QUIET
    and think only thoughts of PEACE
And if I abide in STILLNESS
    my "restless murmurings" cease.

Yesterday... Today... and Tomorrow!

Yesterday's dead,
Tomorrow's unborn,
So there's nothing to fear
And nothing to mourn,
For all that is past
And all that has been
Can never return
To be lived once again—
And what lies ahead
Or the things that will be
Are still in God's Hands
So it is not up to me
To live in the future
That is God's great unknown,
For the past and the present
God claims for His own,
So all I need do
Is to live for Today
And trust God to show me
The Truth and The Way—
For it's only the memory
Of things that have been
And expecting Tomorrow
To bring trouble again
That fills my Today,
Which God wants to bless,
With uncertain fears
And borrowed distress—
For all I need live for
Is this one little minute,
For life's Here and Now
And Eternity's in it.

7

The Windows
of Gold

The Windows of Gold

There is a legend that has often been told
Of the boy who searched for THE WINDOWS OF
  GOLD,
The beautiful windows he saw far away
When he looked in the valley at sunrise each day,
And he yearned to go down to the valley below
But he lived on a mountain that was covered with
  snow
And he knew it would be a difficult trek,
But that was a journey he wanted to make,
So he planned by day and he dreamed by night
Of how he could reach THE GREAT SHINING
  LIGHT . . .
And one golden morning when dawn broke
  through
And the valley sparkled with diamonds of dew
He started to climb down the mountainside
With THE WINDOWS OF GOLD as his goal and
  his guide . . .
He traveled all day and, weary and worn,
With bleeding feet and clothes that were torn
He entered the peaceful valley town
Just as the golden sun went down . . .
But he seemed to have lost his "GUIDING
  LIGHT,"
The windows were dark that had once been bright,
And hungry and tired and lonely and cold
He cried, "WON'T YOU SHOW ME THE WIN-
  DOWS OF GOLD?"
And a kind hand touched him and said, "BEHOLD,
HIGH ON THE MOUNTAIN ARE THE WIN-
  DOWS OF GOLD"—
For the sun going down in a great golden ball
Had burnished the windows of his cabin so small,
And THE KINGDOM OF GOD with its GREAT
  SHINING LIGHT,
Like the Golden Windows that shone so bright,

Is not a far distant place somewhere,
It's as close to you as a silent prayer—
And your search for God will end and begin
When you look for HIM and FIND HIM WITHIN.

Fulfillment

APPLE BLOSSOMS bursting wide
    now beautify the tree
And make a Springtime picture
    that is beautiful to see . . .
Oh, fragrant lovely blossoms,
    you'll make a bright bouquet
If I but break your branches
    from the apple tree today . . .
But if I break your branches
    and make your beauty mine,
You'll bear no fruit in season
    when severed from the vine . . .
And when we cut ourselves away
    from guidance that's divine,
Our lives will be as fruitless
    as the branch without the vine . . .
For as the flowering branches
    depend upon the tree
To nourish and fulfill them
    till they reach futurity,
We too must be dependent
    on our Father up above,
For we are but the BRANCHES
    and He's THE TREE OF LOVE.

"The Heavens Declare the Glory of God"

You ask me how I know it's true
    that there is a living God—
A God who rules the universe,
    the sky . . . the sea . . . the sod;
A God who holds all creatures
    in the hollow of His hand;
A God who put INFINITY
    in one tiny grain of sand;
A God who made the seasons—
    Winter, Summer, Fall and Spring,
And put His flawless rhythm
    into each created thing;
A God who hangs the sun out
    slowly with the break of day,
And gently takes the stars in
    and puts the night away;
A God whose mighty handiwork
    defies the skill of man,
For no architect can alter
    God's PERFECT MASTER PLAN—
What better answers are there
    to prove His Holy Being
Than the wonders all around us
    that are ours just for the seeing.

Ideals Are
Like Stars

In this world of casual carelessness
    it's discouraging to try
To keep our morals and standards
    and our IDEALS HIGH . . .
We are ridiculed and laughed at
    by the smart sophisticate
Who proclaims in brittle banter
    that such things are out of date . . .
But no life is worth the living
    unless it's built on truth,
And we lay our life's foundation
    in the golden years of youth . . .
So allow no one to stop you
    or hinder you from laying
A firm and strong foundation
    made of FAITH AND LOVE AND
      PRAYING . . .
And remember that IDEALS
    are like STARS UP IN THE SKY,
You can never really reach them,
    hanging in the heavens high . . .
But like the mighty mariner
    who sailed the storm-tossed sea,
And used the STARS TO CHART HIS COURSE
    with skill and certainty,
You too can CHART YOUR COURSE IN LIFE
    with HIGH IDEALS AND LOVE,
For HIGH IDEALS ARE LIKE THE STARS
    that light the sky above . . .
You cannot ever reach them,
    but LIFT YOUR HEART UP HIGH
And your LIFE will be as SHINING
    as the STARS UP IN THE SKY.

A Child's Faith

"Jesus loves me, this I know,
For the BIBLE tells me so"—
Little children ask no more,
For love is all they're looking for,
And in a small child's shining eyes
The FAITH of all the ages lies
And tiny hands and tousled heads
That kneel in prayer by little beds
Are closer to the dear Lord's heart
And of His Kingdom more a part
Than we who search, and never find,
The answers to our questioning mind
For FAITH in things we cannot see
Requires a child's simplicity
For, lost in life's complexities,
We drift upon uncharted seas
And slowly FAITH disintegrates
While wealth and power accumulates—
And the more man learns, the less he knows,
And the more involved his thinking grows
And, in his arrogance and pride,
No longer is man satisfied
To place his confidence and love
With childlike FAITH in God above—
Oh, Father, grant once more to men
A simple childlike FAITH again
And, with a small child's trusting eyes,
May all men come to realize
That FAITH alone can save man's soul
And lead him to a HIGHER GOAL.

God Is Never
Beyond Our Reach

No one ever sought the Father
And found HE was not THERE,
And no burden is too heavy
To be lightened by a prayer,
No problem is too intricate
And no sorrow that we face
Is too deep and devastating
To be softened by His grace,
No trials and tribulations
Are beyond what we can bear
If we share them with OUR FATHER
As we talk to HIM in prayer—
And men of every color,
Every race and every creed
Have but to seek the Father
In their deepest hour of need—
God asks for no credentials,
He accepts us with our flaws,
He is kind and understanding
And He welcomes us because
We are His erring children
And He loves us everyone,
And He freely and completely
Forgives all that we have done,
Asking only if we're ready
To follow WHERE HE LEADS—
Content that in His wisdom
He will answer all our needs.

We Can't...
but God Can!

Why things happen as they do
We do not always know,
And we cannot always fathom
Why our spirits sink so low . . .
We flounder in our dark distress,
We are wavering and unstable,
But when we're most inadequate
The Lord God's ALWAYS ABLE . . .
For though we are incapable,
God's powerful and great,
And there's no darkness of the mind
That God can't penetrate . . .
And all that is required of us
Whenever things go wrong
Is to trust in God implicitly
With a FAITH that's deep and strong,
And while He may not instantly
Unravel all the strands
Of the tangled thoughts that trouble us—
He completely understands . . .
And in His time, if we have FAITH,
He will gradually restore
The brightness to our spirit
That we've been longing for . . .
So remember, there's no cloud too dark
For God's light to penetrate
If we keep on believing
And have FAITH ENOUGH to WAIT!

Not by Chance nor Happenstance

Into our lives come many things
    to break the dull routine,
The things we had not planned on
    that happen unforeseen,
The unexpected little joys
    that are scattered on our way,
Success we did not count on
    or a rare, fulfilling day—
A catchy, lilting melody
    that makes us want to dance,
A nameless exaltation
    of enchantment and romance—
An unsought word of kindness,
    a compliment or two
That sets the eyes to gleaming
    like crystal drops of dew—
The unplanned sudden meeting
    that comes with sweet surprise
And lights the heart with happiness
    like a rainbow in the skies . . .
Now some folks call it fickle fate
    and some folks call it chance,
While others just accept it
    as a pleasant happenstance—
But no matter what you call it,
    it didn't come without design,
For all our lives are fashioned
    by the HAND THAT IS DIVINE—
And every happy happening
    and every lucky break
Are little gifts from God above
    that are ours to freely take.

Let Us Seek God's Guidance Through the Year

As the threatening "CLOUDS OF CHAOS"
Gather in man's muddled mind
While he searches for an answer
He alone can never find,
May God turn our vision skyward
So that we can see above
The gathering clouds of darkness
And behold God's brightening love—
For today we're facing problems
Man alone can never solve,
For it takes much more than genius
To determine and resolve
The conditions that confront us
All around on every side,
Daily mounting in intensity
Like the restless, rising tide—
But we'll find new strength and wisdom
If instead of proud resistance
We humbly call upon the Lord
And seek DIVINE ASSISTANCE,
For the spirit can unravel
Many tangled, knotted threads
That defy the skill and power
Of the world's best hands and heads—
For tne plans of growth and progress
Of which we all have dreamed
Cannot survive materially
Unless THE SPIRIT is redeemed—
So as another new year dawns
Let us seek the Lord in prayer
And place our future hopes and plans
Securely in God's care.

8

The Light
of the World

Where Can We Find Him?

Where can we find THE HOLY ONE?
Where can we see HIS ONLY SON?
The Wise Men asked, and we're asking still,
WHERE CAN WE FIND THIS MAN OF
   GOOD WILL?
Is He far away in some distant place,
Ruling unseen from His throne of grace?
Is there nothing on earth that man can see
To give him proof of ETERNITY?

It's true we have never looked on His face,
But His likeness shines forth from every place,
For THE HAND OF GOD is everywhere
Along life's busy thoroughfare . . .
And His presence can be felt and seen
Right in the midst of our daily routine,
The things we touch and see and feel
Are what make God so very real . . .

The silent stars in timeless skies,
The wonderment in children's eyes,
The gossamer wings of a hummingbird,
The joy that comes from a kindly word . . .
The Autumn haze, the breath of Spring,
The chirping song the crickets sing,
A rosebud in a slender vase,
A smile upon a friendly face . . .

In everything both great and small
We see THE HAND OF GOD IN ALL,
And every day, somewhere, someplace,
We see THE LIKENESS OF HIS FACE . . .
For who can watch a new day's birth
Or touch the warm, life-giving earth,

Or feel the softness of the breeze
Or look at skies through lacy trees
And say they've never seen His face
Or looked upon His throne of grace!

"Unto Us a Child Is Born"

God sent the little Christ Child
So man might understand
"That a little child shall lead them"
To that unknown "PROMISED LAND" . . .
For God in His great wisdom
Knew that men would rise to power
And forget HIS HOLY PRECEPTS
In their great triumphal hour . . .
He knew that they would question
And doubt the Holy Birth
And turn their time and talents
To the pleasures of this earth . . .
But every new discovery
Is an open avenue
To more and greater mysteries,
And man's search is never through . . .
For man can never fathom
The mysteries of the Lord
Or understand His promise
Of a heavenly reward . . .
For no one but a LITTLE CHILD
With simple FAITH and LOVE
Can lead man's straying footsteps
To HIGHER REALMS ABOVE!

He Was One of Us

He was born as little children are
    and lived as children do,
So remember that the Saviour
    was once a child like you,
And remember that He lived on earth
    in the midst of sinful men,
And the problems of the present
    existed even then;
He was ridiculed and laughed at
    in the same heartbreaking way
That we who fight for justice
    are ridiculed today;
He was tempted . . . He was hungry . . .
    He was lonely . . . He was sad . . .
There's no sorrowful experience
    that the Saviour has not had;
And in the end he was betrayed
    and even crucified,
For He was truly "ONE OF US"—
    He lived on earth and died;
So do not heed the skeptics
    who are often heard to say:
"WHAT DOES GOD UP IN HEAVEN
    KNOW OF THINGS WE FACE
      TODAY" . . .
For, our Father up in heaven
    is very much aware
Of our failures and shortcomings
    and the burdens that we bear;
So whenever you are troubled
    put your problems in God's Hand
For He has faced all problems
    AND HE WILL UNDERSTAND.

In the Garden
of Gethsemane

Before the dawn of Easter
There came Gethsemane . . .
Before the Resurrection
There were hours of agony . . .
For there can be no crown of stars
Without a cross to bear,
And there is no salvation
Without FAITH and LOVE and PRAYER,
And when we take our needs to God
Let us pray as did His Son
That dark night in Gethsemane—
"THY WILL, NOT MINE, BE DONE."

"Why Should He
Die for Such as I"

In everything both great and small
We see the Hand of God in all,
And in the miracles of Spring
When EVERYWHERE in EVERYTHING
His handiwork is all around
And every lovely sight and sound
Proclaims the GOD of earth and sky
I ask myself "JUST WHO AM I"
That God should send His only Son
That my salvation would be won
Upon a CROSS by a sinless man
To bring fulfillment to God's Plan—
For Jesus suffered, bled and died
That sinners might be sanctified,
And to grant God's children SUCH AS I
Eternal life in that HOME on HIGH.

The Way of the Cross Leads to God

He carried the cross to Calvary,
Carried its burden for you and me,
There on the cross He was crucified
And, because He suffered and bled and died,
We know that whatever "OUR CROSS" may be,
It leads to GOD and ETERNITY . . .
For who can hope for a "crown of stars"
Unless it is earned with suffering and scars,
For how could we face the living Lord
And rightfully claim His promised reward
If we have not carried our cross of care
And tasted the cup of bitter despair . . .
Let those who yearn for the pleasures of life,
And long to escape all suffering and strife,
Rush recklessly on to an "empty goal"
With never a thought of the spirit and soul . . .
But if you are searching to find the way
To life everlasting and eternal day—
With Faith in your heart take the path He trod,
For the WAY OF THE CROSS is the WAY TO
    GOD.

"I Know That My Redeemer Liveth"

They asked me how I know it's true
That the Saviour lived and died . . .
And if I believe the story
That the Lord was crucified?
And I have so many answers
To prove His Holy Being,
Answers that are everywhere
Within the realm of seeing . . .
The leaves that fell at autumn
And were buried in the sod
Now budding on the tree boughs
To lift their arms to God . . .
The flowers that were covered
And entombed beneath the snow
Pushing through the "darkness"
To bid the Spring "hello" . . .
On every side Great Nature
Retells the Easter Story—
So who am I to question
"The Resurrection Glory."

In God Is Our Strength

It's a troubled world we live in
    and we wish that we might find
Not only happiness of heart
    but longed-for peace of mind—

But where can we begin our search
    in the age of automation
With neighbor against neighbor
    and nation against nation—

Where values have no permanence
    and change is all around
And everything is "sinking sand"
    and nothing "solid ground"—

Have we placed our faith in leaders
    unworthy of our trust?
Have we lost our own identity
    and allowed our souls to rust?

Have we forgotten Babylon
    and Egypt, Rome and Greece
And all the mighty rulers
    who lived by war, not peace,

Who built their thrones and empires
    on power and man-made things
And never knew God's Greatness
    or that He was KING OF KINGS?

But we've God's Easter Promise,
    so let us seek a goal
That opens up new vistas
    for man's eternal soul—

For our strength and our security
    lie not in earthly things,
But in CHRIST THE LORD who died for us
    and rose as KING OF KINGS.

"I Am the Way, the Truth and the Life"

I AM THE WAY
  so just follow ME
Though the way be rough
  and you cannot see . . .

I AM THE TRUTH
  which all men seek
So heed not "false prophets"
  nor the words that they speak . . .

I AM THE LIFE
  and I hold the key
That opens the door
  to ETERNITY . . .

And in this dark world
  I AM THE LIGHT
To THE PROMISED LAND
  WHERE THERE IS NO NIGHT!

"I Am the Light of the World"

Oh, Father, up in heaven,
We have wandered far away
From Jesus Christ, Our Saviour,
Who arose on Easter Day . . .
And the promise of salvation
That God gave us when Christ died
We have often vaguely questioned,
Even doubted and denied . . .
We've forgotten why You sent us
Jesus Christ Your Only Son,
And in arrogance and ignorance—
It's OUR WILL, not THINE, BE DONE . . .
Oh, shed THY LIGHT upon us
As Easter dawns this year,
And may we feel THE PRESENCE
Of the RISEN SAVIOUR near . . .
And, God, in Thy great wisdom,
Lead us in the way that's right,
And may "THE DARKNESS" of this world
Be conquered by "THY LIGHT."

9

Life Is Forever

Life Is Forever!
Death Is a Dream!

If we did not go to sleep at night
We'd never awaken to see the light,
And the joy of watching a new day break
Or meeting the dawn by some quiet lake
Would never be ours unless we slept
While God and all His angels kept
A vigil through this "little death"
That's over with the morning's breath—
And death, too, is a time of sleeping,
For those who die are in God's keeping
And there's a "sunrise" for each soul,
For LIFE not DEATH is God's promised goal—
So trust God's promise and doubt Him never
For only through death can man LIVE FOREVER!

I Do Not Go Alone

If DEATH should beckon me with outstretched hand
And whisper softly of "AN UNKNOWN LAND,"
I shall not be afraid to go,
For though the path I do not know,
I take DEATH'S HAND without a fear,
For He who safely brought me here
Will also take me safely back,
And though in many things I lack,
He will not let me go alone
Into the "VALLEY THAT'S UNKNOWN" . . .
So I reach out and take DEATH'S HAND
And journey to the "PROMISED LAND!"

104

The End of the Road Is But a Bend in the Road

When we feel we have nothing left to give
    and we are sure that the "song has ended"—
When our day seems over and the shadows fall
    and the darkness of night has descended,
Where can we go to find the strength
    to valiantly keep on trying,
Where can we find the hand that will dry
    the tears that the heart is crying—
There's but one place to go and that is to God
    and, dropping all pretense and pride,
We can pour out our problems without restraint
    and gain strength with Him at our side—
And together we stand at life's crossroads
    and view what we think is the end,
But God has a much bigger vision
    and He tells us it's ONLY A BEND—
For the road goes on and is smoother,
    and the "pause in the song" is a "rest,"
And the part that's unsung and unfinished
    is the sweetest and richest and best—
So rest and relax and grow stronger,
    LET GO and LET GOD share your load,
Your work is not finished or ended,
    you've just come to "A BEND IN THE
    ROAD."

Spring Awakens What Autumn Puts to Sleep

A garden of asters of varying hues,
Crimson-pinks and violet-blues,
Blossoming in the hazy Fall
Wrapped in Autumn's lazy pall—
But early frost stole in one night
And like a chilling, killing blight
It touched each pretty aster's head
And now the garden's still and dead
And all the lovely flowers that bloomed
Will soon be buried and entombed
In Winter's icy shroud of snow
But oh, how wonderful to know
That after Winter comes the Spring
To breathe new life in everything,
And all the flowers that fell in death
Will be awakened by Spring's breath—
For in God's Plan both men and flowers
Can only reach "bright, shining hours"
By dying first to rise in glory
And prove again the Easter Story.

Death Is a Doorway

On the "WINGS of DEATH"
    the "SOUL takes FLIGHT"
Into the land where
    "THERE IS NO NIGHT"—
For those who believe
    what the Saviour said
Will rise in glory
    though they be dead . . .
So death comes to us
    just to "OPEN THE DOOR"
To the KINGDOM OF GOD
    and LIFE EVERMORE.

There's Always a Springtime

After the Winter comes the Spring
To show us again that in everything
There's always renewal divinely planned,
Flawlessly perfect, the work of God's Hand . . .
And just like the seasons that come and go
When the flowers of Spring lay buried in snow,
God sends to the heart in its winter of sadness
A springtime awakening of new hope and gladness,
And loved ones who sleep in a season of death
Will, too, be awakened by God's life-giving breath.

The Legend of the Raindrop

The legend of the raindrop
    has a lesson for us all
As it trembled in the heavens
    questioning whether it should fall—
For the glistening raindrop argued
    to the genie of the sky,
"I am beautiful and lovely
    as I sparkle here on high,
And hanging here I will become
    part of the rainbow's hue
And I'll shimmer like a diamond
    for all the world to view" . . .
But the genie told the raindrop,
    "Do not hesitate to go,
For you will be more beautiful
    if you fall to earth below,
For you will sink into the soil
    and be lost a while from sight,
But when you reappear on earth,
    you'll be looked on with delight;
For you will be the raindrop
    that quenched the thirsty ground
And helped the lovely flowers
    to blossom all around,
And in your resurrection
    you'll appear in queenly clothes
With the beauty of the lily
    and the fragrance of the rose;
Then, when you wilt and wither,
    you'll become part of the earth
And make the soil more fertile
    and give new flowers birth" . . .
For there is nothing ever lost
    or ETERNALLY NEGLECTED,
For EVERYTHING GOD EVER MADE
    IS ALWAYS RESURRECTED;

So trust God's all-wise wisdom
        and doubt the Father never,
For in HIS HEAVENLY KINGDOM
        THERE IS NOTHING LOST FOREVER.

"Because He Lives... We too Shall Live"

In this restless world of struggle
        it is very hard to find
Answers to the questions
        that daily come to mind—
We cannot see the future,
        what's beyond is still unknown,
For the secret of God's Kingdom
        still belongs to Him alone—
But He granted us salvation
        when His Son was crucified,
For life became immortal
        because our Saviour died.

When I Must Leave You

When I must leave you
    for a little while,
Please do not grieve
    and shed wild tears
And hug your sorrow
    to you through the years,
But start out bravely
    with a gallant smile;
And for my sake
    and in my name
Live on and do
    all things the same,
Feed not your loneliness
    on empty days,
But fill each waking hour
    in useful ways,
Reach out your hand
    in comfort and in cheer
And I in turn will comfort you
    and hold you near;
And never, never
    be afraid to die,
For I am waiting
    for you in the sky!

Each Spring, God Renews His Promise

Long, long ago in a land far away,
There came the dawn of the first Easter Day,
And each year we see that promise reborn
That God gave the world on that first Easter Morn . . .
For in each waking flower and each singing bird,
The Promise of Easter is witnessed and heard,
And Spring is God's way of speaking to men
And renewing the promise of Easter again,
For death is a season that man must pass through
And, just like the flowers, God wakens him, too . . .
So why should we grieve when our loved ones die,
For we'll meet them again in a "cloudless sky"—
For Easter is more than a beautiful story,
It's the promise of life and Eternal Glory.

Death Is Only a Part of Life

We enter this world
  from "THE GREAT UNKNOWN"
And GOD gives each SPIRIT
  a form of its own
And endows this form
  with a heart and a soul
To spur man on
  to his ultimate goal . . .
For all men are born
  to RETURN as they CAME
And birth and death
  are in essence the same
And man is but born
  to die and arise
For beyond this world
  in beauty there lies
The purpose of death
  which is but to gain
LIFE EVERLASTING
  in GOD'S GREAT DOMAIN . . .
And no one need make
  this journey alone
For GOD has promised
  to take care of HIS own.

On the Other Side of Death

Death is a GATEWAY
 we all must pass through
To reach that Fair Land
 where the soul's born anew,
For man's born to die
 and his sojourn on earth
Is a short span of years
 beginning with birth . . .
And like pilgrims we wander
 until death takes our hand
And we start on our journey
 to God's Promised Land,
A place where we'll find
 no suffering nor tears,
Where TIME is not counted
 by days, months or years . . .
And in this Fair City
 that God has prepared
Are unending joys
 to be happily shared
With all of our loved ones
 who patiently wait
On Death's Other Side
 to open "THE GATE"!

Death Opens the Door to Life Evermore

We live a short while on earth below,
Reluctant to die for we do not know
Just what "dark death" is all about
And so we view it with fear and doubt
Not certain of what is around the bend
We look on death as the final end
To all that made us a mortal being
And yet there lies just beyond our seeing
A beautiful life so full and complete
That we should leave with hurrying feet
To walk with God by sacred streams
Amid beauty and peace beyond our dreams—
For all who believe in the RISEN LORD
Have been assured of this reward
And death for them is just "graduation"
To a higher realm of wide elevation—
For life on earth is a transient affair,
Just a few brief years in which to prepare
For a life that is free from pain and tears
Where time is not counted by hours or years—
For death is only the method God chose
To colonize heaven with the souls of those
Who by their apprenticeship on earth
Proved worthy to dwell in the land of new birth—
So death is not sad . . . it's a time for elation,
A joyous transition . . . .. the soul's emigration
Into a place where the soul's SAFE and FREE
To live with God through ETERNITY!

10

God Bless America

God Bless America

"AMERICA THE BEAUTIFUL"—
May it always stay that way—
But to keep "OLD GLORY" flying
There's a price that we must pay . . .
For everything worth having
Demands work and sacrifice,
And FREEDOM is a GIFT from God
That commands the HIGHEST PRICE . . .
For all our wealth and progress
Are as worthless as can be
Without the FAITH that made us great
And kept OUR COUNTRY FREE . . .
Nor can our nation hope to live
Unto itself alone,
For the problems of our neighbors
Must today become our own . . .
And while it's hard to understand
The complexities of war,
Each one of us must realize
That we are fighting for
The principles of freedom
And the decency of man,
And as a Christian Nation
We're committed to God's Plan . . .
And as the LAND OF LIBERTY
And a great God-fearing nation
We must protect our honor
And fulfill our obligation . . .
So in these times of crisis
Let us offer no resistance
In giving help to those who need
Our strength and our assistance—
And "THE STARS AND STRIPES FOREVER"
Will remain a symbol of
A rich and mighty nation
Built on FAITH and TRUTH and LOVE.

A Prayer for Peace

Our Father, up in heaven,
     hear this fervent prayer—
May the people of ALL NATIONS
     BE UNITED IN THY CARE,
For earth's peace and man's salvation
     can come only by Thy grace
And not through bombs and missiles
     and our quest for outer space . . .
For until all men recognize
     that "THE BATTLE IS THE LORD'S"
And peace on earth cannot be won
     with strategy and swords,
We will go on vainly fighting,
     as we have in ages past,
Finding only empty victories
     and a peace that cannot last . . .
But we've grown so rich and mighty
     and so arrogantly strong,
We no longer ask in humbleness—
     "God, show us where we're wrong" . . .
We have come to trust completely
     in the power of man-made things,
Unmindful of God's mighty power
     and that HE IS "KING OF KINGS" . . .
We have turned our eyes away from HIM
     to go our selfish way,
And money, power and pleasure
     are the gods we serve today . . .
And the good green earth God gave us
     to peacefully enjoy,
Through greed and fear and hatred
     we are seeking to destroy . . .
Oh, Father, up in heaven,
     stir and wake our sleeping souls,
Renew our faith and lift us up
     and give us higher goals,
And grant us heavenly guidance
     as war threatens us again—
For, more than GUIDED MISSILES,
     all the world needs GUIDED MEN.

A Memorial Day Prayer

They SERVED and FOUGHT and DIED
    so that we might be SAFE and FREE,
Grant them, O LORD, ETERNAL PEACE
    and give them "THE VICTORY"!
And in these days of unrest,
    filled with grave uncertainty,
Let's not forget THE PRICE THEY PAID
    to keep OUR COUNTRY FREE . . .
And so, on this MEMORIAL DAY,
    we offer up a prayer—
May the people of ALL NATIONS
    be UNITED in THY CARE,
And grant us understanding
    and teach us how to live
So we may lose our selfish pride
    and learn to love and give,
And keep us ever mindful
    of the fighting men who sleep
In Arlington and foreign lands
    so we may ever keep
The "light of freedom" burning
    in their honor through the years
And hear their cry for PEACE ON EARTH
    resounding in our ears—
Forgive us our transgressions
    and "Oh, God, be with us yet"
Lest in our pride and arrogance
    we heedlessly FORGET.

In God We Trust

O God, our Help in Ages Past,
    our Hope in Years To Be,
Look down upon this PRESENT
    and see our need of THEE—
For in this age of unrest,
    with danger all around,
We need Thy hand to lead us
    to higher, safer ground,
We need Thy help and counsel
    to make us more aware
That our safety and security
    lie solely in Thy care—
And as we FIGHT FOR FREEDOM
    make our way and purpose clear
And in our hours of danger
    may we feel Thy Presence near.

In Times Like These

We read the headlines daily
　　and listen to the news,
We shake our heads despairingly
　　and glumly sing the blues—
We are restless and dissatisfied
　　and we do not feel secure,
We are vaguely discontented
　　with the things we must endure . . .
This violent age we live in
　　is filled with nameless fears
As we listen to the newscasts
　　that come daily to our ears,
And we view the threatening future
　　with sad sobriety
As we're surrounded daily
　　by increased anxiety . . .
How can we find security
　　or stand on solid ground
When there's violence and dissension
　　and confusion all around;
Where can we go for refuge
　　from the rising tides of hate,

Where can we find a haven
    to escape this shameful fate . . .
So instead of reading headlines
    that disturb the heart and mind,
Let us open up the BIBLE
    and in doing so we'll find
That this age is no different
    from the millions gone before,
But in every hour of crisis
    God has opened up a door
For all who seek His guidance
    and trust His all-wise plan,
For God provides protection
    beyond that devised by man . . .
And we learn that each TOMORROW
    is not ours to understand,
But lies safely in the keeping
    of the great Creator's Hand,
And to have the steadfast knowledge
    that WE NEVER WALK ALONE
And to rest in the assurance
    that our EVERY NEED IS KNOWN
Will help dispel our worries,
    our anxieties and care,
For doubt and fear are vanquished
    in THE PEACEFULNESS OF PRAYER.

Keep America in Your Care

We are faced with many problems
  that grow bigger day by day
And, as we seek to solve them
  in our own self-sufficient way,
We keep drifting into chaos
  and our avarice and greed
Blinds us to the answer
  that would help us in our need . . .
Oh, God, renew our spirit
  and make us more aware
That our future is dependent
  on sacrifice and prayer,
Forgive us our transgressions
  and revive our faith anew
So we may all draw closer
  to each other and to You . . .
For when a nation is too proud
  to daily kneel and pray
It will crumble into chaos
  and descend into decay,
So stir us with compassion
  and raise our standards higher
And take away our lust for power
  and make our one desire
To be a SHINING SYMBOL
  of ALL THAT'S GREAT AND GOOD
As You lead us in our struggle
  toward NEW-FOUND BROTHERHOOD!

This I Believe

Somehow the world seems to be most deeply concerned and curiously interested in "WHO WE ARE." But "WHO WE ARE" is of such small importance to GOD, for HIS deep concern is with "WHAT WE ARE." And complete and full knowledge of "WHAT WE ARE" is known to GOD alone, for man's small, shallow judgments are so empty of the GOODNESS and GREATNESS of GOD'S MERCIFUL LOVE. And while man's motives and missions, his programs and projects, and his accomplishments and acclaim can make him successful and secure for him a listing in "WHO'S WHO," he remains UNLISTED in GOD'S "WHO'S WHO," for great is the power of might and mind . . . BUT ONLY LOVE CAN MAKE US KIND . . . and all we are or hope to be . . . is empty pride and vanity . . . if love is not a part of all . . . THE GREATEST MAN IS VERY SMALL!

I am a very simple, uncomplicated person, and I possess only a CHILD'S FAITH, which completely answers all of my questions, satisfies all my longings, and never prompts me to seek a detailed explanation of how GOD works or to make a scientific study of HIS methods and HIS motives.

When I attended Sunday school, which is now much more than half a century ago, I used to sing, with all the joy that a child's heart can hold, "JESUS LOVES ME," for I knew HE loved me then and that HE would love me forever. This same knowledge still suffices to fill me with THE SAME CHILDLIKE FAITH I possessed then, for I believe only a child can really know the GREATNESS OF GOD'S LOVE. I think that in searching and studying and using our man-made theories, we tend to destroy the POWER, the GLORY, the GREATNESS, and, most of all, the "INCOMPREHENSIBLE MIRACLE" of GOD and HIS SON.

I ask for no sensational, spectacular evidence or proof that GOD is MY FATHER and that HIS SON, JESUS, LOVES ME. I only know that HE who brought me into this world will also take me safely back . . . for though there are many things I lack . . . HE will not let me go alone . . . into a land that is unknown. And with that knowledge I can travel happily on "THE HIGHWAY TO HEAVEN" and always with "hurrying feet," for I know GOD will open "new fields of usefulness" for me, where there are no limitations, no handicaps, and no restrictions.

My outlook on life is just the simple outlook faith provides for each one of us if we do not attempt to remake GOD into a GOD OF OUR OWN SPECIFICATIONS, who meets our own selfish needs.

And never think of GOD as something apart, for HE is really a part of our heart. HE is not in a far-away place but only a prayer away. And just because we cannot touch HIS HAND and see HIS FACE does not mean that HE is not beside us at all times. Remember, you cannot see the air or capture it with your hand, but you can feel a gentle breeze on a sunny day or the wind's powerful blast in the fury of the storm, and you know without breathing this air you would die, for like GOD, it is truly "THE BREATH OF LIFE."

I just know everything that has ever happened in my life, whether it was good or bad, glad or sad, GOD sent it for a reason, and I truly believe with all my heart that "GOD NEVER MAKES MISTAKES." I never question what GOD sends, for I realize, when you question GOD, you lose the UNQUESTIONABLE POWER OF FAITH and you no longer can enjoy its endless benefits.

I pray constantly, not always on my knees or at special places or at special times, nor do I use impressive words. I just keep up a running conversation with GOD, hour by hour and day by day. I talk to HIM about everything, and I ask HIM for nothing, except the joy of knowing HIM better and loving HIM more.

I am not "ritualistically religious" or "denominationally directed," and when columnists question me, I just answer with this quote from one of my poems:

> "Ask me not my race or creed . . . just take me in my hour of need . . . and let me know YOU love me, too . . . and that I am a part of YOU . . . for in THE HOLY FATHER'S SIGHT . . . no man is yellow, black, or white."

And I feel that every man has a deep "heart need" that cannot be filled with doctrine or creed, for the soul of man knows nothing more than just that he is longing for a haven that is safe and sure and a fortress where he feels secure.

It is true my poems have had phenomenal sales wherever they have been made available. They are read by all creeds, all classes, all colors, all ages, and in all countries, and the people who read my writings identify with them because GOD is really a part of every heart in the world and *IT IS GOD TALKING* and not me.

I never think of myself as a success or as an author or a poet. I only think of myself as another "worker" in "GOD'S VINEYARD." The phenomenal sale of my books and writings is not due to anything special about me or my way of living. It is just because people all over the world, under GOD'S DIRECTION, have seen their own souls reflected in the words I have borrowed from GOD.

When people write, telephone, or cable to come and see me, I strongly discourage them, because they do not realize that in meeting me, they are just meeting themselves, for the same GOD who abides in them abides in me and HE reaches from heart to heart. TIME and SPACE mean nothing when GOD TAKES OVER, for all physical and material limitations fade before the POWER of SPIRITUAL REALITY.

All my verses are "woven" from "the silken strands of thought" provided in the letters I receive and the conversations I have with people. For no matter how we mask our feelings outwardly, we all at some time experience the same many-faceted emotions that come to all mankind, often unwelcomed, unsought, unwanted, and unheralded, and no matter how adept man is at disguising what he really is inside, we all do share these same human emotions. We are all lonely, but we are never alone . . . for GOD is our FATHER and we are HIS OWN . . . we are all subject to trials and tribulation . . . but we are always welcome to seek GOD in meditation . . . we are all disappointed and have hours of despair . . . but we always have access to our FATHER in prayer . . . and all we ever have to do is to "LET GO and LET GOD!"

All our troubles and problems, as individuals or as a nation, stem from our incurable, unconquerable curiosity and our grim determination to find out "WHO" or "WHAT" CREATED CREATION and we all aspire to find out "WHO GOD REALLY IS." We are constantly seeking and searching for NEW WAYS to solve OLD PROBLEMS without giving FAITH a real chance. We have FAITH, but we do not have ENOUGH FAITH, and man cannot bring himself to "lose himself in the LOVE of GOD."

All these "OLDEN GOLDEN TRUTHS" that are constantly repeated through the ages just substantiate the MAJESTIC TRUTH of ECCLESIASTES, for "THERE IS NOTHING NEW UNDER THE SUN." Everything that has been before will be again, for as long as there are selfish, greedy, arrogant men who think they can outmaneuver, outguess, outdo, and outmanipulate GOD, they will never find the solution to the problems on earth. So, the SEASONS come and the SEASONS go . . . and the RIVERS flow and the WINDS still blow . . . and GOD still smiles and watches man . . . knowing always "MAN CAN'T but HE CAN!"

I am well aware that I cannot make it on my own, and I ask GOD to take my hand and hold it tight, for I cannot walk alone. Each day GOD only asks us to do our best, and then HE will take over and do all the rest. And remember, GOD is always available and ready to help anyone who asks HIM, for GOD is HERE . . . HE'S THERE . . . HE'S EVERYWHERE . . . HE'S as close to you as HE is to me . . . and wherever you are GOD is sure to be. And I want you to know that the poems I write are not mine alone . . . they belong to GOD and to the people I've known . . . and while I may

never have met you face-to-face . . . in GOD'S
LOVE and by HIS GRACE . . . our hearts and
minds can meet and share . . . my little poems of
FAITH and PRAYER . . . and though we are
oceans and miles apart . . . GOD unites us in
SPIRIT and HEART!

More of Thee . . . Less of Me

Take me and break me and make me, dear God,
Just what you want me to be—
Give me the strength to accept what you send
And eyes with the vision to see
All the small arrogant ways that I have
And the vain little things that I do,
Make me aware that I'm often concerned
More with MYSELF than with YOU.
Uncover before me my weakness and greed
And help me to search deep inside
So I may discover how easy it is
To be selfishly lost in my pride—
And then in Thy goodness and mercy
Look down on this weak, erring one
And tell me that I am forgiven
For all I've so willfully done.
And teach me to humbly start following
The path that the dear Saviour trod
So I'll find at the end of life's journey
"A HOME IN THE CITY OF GOD."

A Word from the Author
"Just For You"

My heart rejoices and I'm thankful, too,
That I could share this book with you
For this book is truly a "GIFT of LOVE"
For all my poems are woven of
Words I borrow from Our Father Above
For this is a "PARTNERSHIP of THREE,"
GOD FIRST, then YOU, and last of all ME . . .
For I'm not an author writing for fame
Seeking new laurels or praise for my name,
I am only a "worker" employed by the Lord
And great is my gladness and rich my reward
If I can just spread the wonderful story
That GOD is the ANSWER to ETERNAL
    GLORY . . .
And only the people who read my poems
Can help me to reach more HEARTS and HOMES,
Bringing new hope and comfort and cheer,
Telling sad hearts there is nothing to fear
And what greater joy could there be than to share
The LOVE of GOD and the POWER of PRAYER!

May GOD'S LOVE and HIS JOY flow around
this troubled world and may YOU and I
together help to make this a REALITY. This
is the wish and the prayer of